my first

Day of the Dead

Picture Book

This book belongs to:

_____

Altar

Offrenda

Bread of the Dead

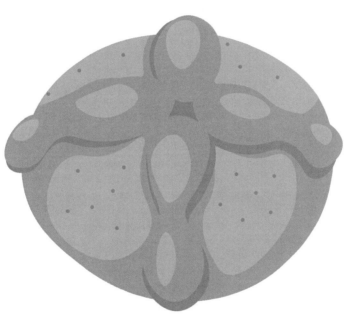

Pan de Muerto

Cemetery

Cementerio

Pictures

Fotografías

Sugar Skulls

Calaveras

Marigolds

Caléndulas

Guitar

Guitarra

Mole

Mole

Skeletons

Esqueletos

Catrinas

Catrinas

Snacks

Meriendas

Candles

Velas

Mexico

México

Little Angels

Angelitos

Fruit

Frutas

Kukulkan

Kukulkan

Banner

Papel Picado

Golletes

Golletes

Cross

Cruz

Children

HOLA

Niños

AncestorS

AncestroS

Party

Fiesta

Music

Música

Incense

Incienso

Cinnamon

Canela

Religion

Religión

Happy Day of the Dead!

¡Feliz Día de los Muertos!

Made in United States
North Haven, CT
12 October 2023

42648339R10018